RICHARD W. BAGSHAWE

MA, CEng, MIMechE

ROMAN ROADS

SHIRE ARCHAEOLOGY

Published in 1994 by
SHIRE PUBLICATIONS LTD
Cromwell House, Church Street, Princes Risborough,
Buckinghamshire HP27 9AJ, UK.

Series Editor: James Dyer

ISBN 0 85263 458 7

First published 1979; reprinted 1982, 1985, 1990 and 1994.

Printed in Great Britain by
CIT Printing Services, Press Buildings,
Merlins Bridge, Haverfordwest, Dyfed SA61 1XF.

Contents

List of illustrations

The figures

Preface

It is not possible within the confines of this book to deal with Roman roads in great depth, but an attempt has been made to introduce the reader to a fascinating subject towards which he or she could make a contribution if so desired. Advice as to how this may be achieved is given after covering the archaeological and historical aspects, and books for further reading are suggested in the select bibliography.

The publishers have provided for the use of more half-tone plates for purposes of illustration than in any other comparable work, so that the reader should know precisely what to look for in the field under present conditions.

Apart from the aerial photographs, which were initially selected by the staff of Aerofilms Ltd, and the three reproductions of early maps it may be assumed that, where a photograph is not credited otherwise, it was taken by the present author in the course of fieldwork. Thanks are due to the other photographers for permission to use their work.

The author is also grateful for professional help in various forms from the following: W. H. Brooker, Arthur Dawes, Alan Gray, Brian King and Mrs Lillian Kerr, who undertook the irksome task of typing and retyping the manuscript as required. The series editor, James Dyer, has been most painstaking over giving clear guidance in preparing this work.

Some Roman roads are mentioned or depicted for the first time, being the result of recent discoveries. Nevertheless, in no case has new material been used in this book which did not have the approval of the late Mr I. D. Margary, MA, FSA, to whom the present author owes the greatest debt, which can never be repaid.

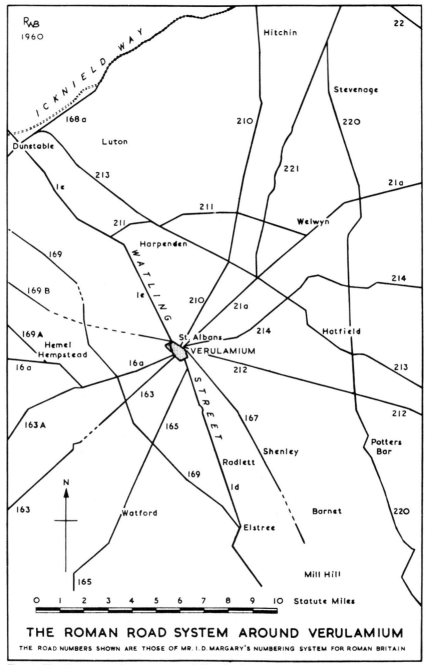

Fig. 1. The Roman road system around Verulamium.

1
Introduction

The Romans are supposed to have learned the rudimentary art of road construction from the Etruscans. Rome itself is said to have been founded in 753 BC. By 312 BC the censor Appius Claudius had laid out and given his name to the old Appian Way which ran south-south-east from the Porta Appia (now the gateway of San Sebastiano) on the approximate line of an earlier trackway to the Albani Hills. This paved road was the first and most spectacular of the consular roads (*Regina Viarum*) and was followed by others leading out of Rome such as the Via Flaminia, Via Aurelia, Via Praenestina, Via Salaria (Salt Way) and Via Nomentana, to name but a few of more than a dozen so far known.

As Roman military power penetrated northwards and took over Gaul, Spain and eventually the province of Britannia in AD 43 under the Emperor Claudius, so the skills of the legionary road builders improved, reaching their zenith in England, Wales and part of Scotland by about AD 80.

An approximate estimate of the total mileage in Britain would be about 10,000 miles (16,000 km), based on 7,400 miles (11,900 km) of known roads and perhaps another 2,000 miles (3,000 km) still to be found. This was achieved during the first century of the occupation and one mile of road produced on average in about three to four days constantly for one hundred years is a superb record by any standards.

The word 'mile' is derived from the Latin *milia passuum,* meaning one thousand paces. Since one pace was what we would call two steps, left and right, the length of a Roman mile works out at 1,680 yards (1,536m) compared with the 1,760 yards (1,609m) of a statute mile.

Because of the conformity to a set pattern of behaviour and type of construction throughout Britain, it is useful to imagine that there must have been some kind of military road manual available to the soldiers describing exactly how to do the job in given circumstances, but there is no proof of this.

Furthermore, from archaeological observation it is fairly clear that halfway through the period an instruction came from Rome ordering the surveyors to make economies, and so the later roads were not so direct or so well engineered. It is also probable that there was a transition from military to civil contracting, with later emphasis on commercial and agricultural needs.

But what was the position in Britain before the Claudian invasion? The earliest roads of all were the ridgeways of no defined width or exact position. Professor W. F. Grimes has demonstrated such a ridgeway running along the Jurassic ridge of the Cotswolds. Then there were in the later prehistoric periods routes such as the Icknield Way, which became a band of parallel trackways at the foot of the Chiltern Hills.

There appeared in 1922 a booklet by Alfred Watkins entitled *Early British Trackways,* which was expanded in 1925 into a book, *The Old Straight Track,* that ran into many editions and is still available. His contention was that many significant prehistoric straight alignments or 'leys' existed and could be proved by anyone with good sight, a ruler and a map. All one can say about this without going into too much detail is that it is an extraordinary mixture of expert photography, mistaken etymology, ignorance of map projection and surveying, random selection of objects and features of different periods in time, wrongful attribution of riders' mounting stones, unrecorded Roman roads, odd earthworks, muddled thinking, coincidences and luck to prove a theory no serious archaeologist believes, but which has many adherents.

Of quite a different nature was the work done on prehistoric trackways between the two world wars by, for instance, Dr G. B. Grundy on *Ancient Highways* in Dorset, Somerset, Wiltshire, Berkshire and Hampshire; Drs E. and E. C. Curwen (father and son) on *Covered Ways in the Sussex Downs,* the purpose of which is still puzzling; and Dr. O. G. S. Crawford, the first Archaeological Officer of the Ordnance Survey, who had a wonderful aptitude for sorting wheat from chaff, wrote several books on many aspects of archaeology and was responsible for the first edition of the OS map of Roman Britain. He was certainly not desk-bound. Others included Mr Harold T. Peake, perhaps best known for his knowledge and help given to others, but also for his work on the archaeology of *Berkshire;* Mr R. Hippisley Cox, on *The Green Roads of England,* not so sound an authority as the others; Edward Thomas on *The Icknield Way,* good enough but with too much irrelevant chat, and much the same might be said of the works of Hilaire Belloc.

Three unpaid specialists on Roman roads also deserve mention. They should not be described as 'amateurs' in the derogatory sense, since they were professional men in other fields. The first is the Rev. Thomas Leman (1751-1826), whose priceless and unique manuscripts, covering his journeys on horseback and observations on Roman roads, are preserved in Devizes and Luton museums. He had several associates: Philip Crocker, a surveyor employed by Sir Richard Colt Hoare; Daniel and Samuel Lysons; the Rev. William Bennet, later Bishop of Cloyne; and Dr Charles Mason, who became Rector of Orwell, Cambridgeshire. Not all Victorian clergymen neglected their parishioners as did Leman, but those who took their religious duties seriously, stopped at home and yet wrote about the ancient past were inclined to speculate without first-hand knowledge and field observation.

Much later, in 1903, a civil engineer, Thomas Codrington, decided to put existing knowledge together, albeit incomplete (as it always will be), and wrote the very practical and accurate *Roman Roads in Britain,* which became the standard work on the subject for fifty-two years, until superseded by Ivan Donald Margary's two volumes with the same title. Indeed, at one time Margary said that a rewriting of Codrington could not be done by anyone, but later he did so himself brilliantly.

I. D. Margary was the doyen of Roman road studies; a wealthy land owner, he lived at East Grinstead, West Sussex, and first took an interest in Roman roads by fortunately finding on an air photograph in 1929 traces of an unrecorded Roman road passing through Ashdown Forest. Once he had got the scent of his first Roman road he maintained his interest and gave considerable encouragement to others until his death in 1976. Modest but firm in his opinions, generous to preservationists, he at first covered thoroughly Sussex, Surrey and part of Kent and was also associated with the road system around *Durobrivae* (Water Newton) between 1931 and 1935.

Under the auspices of the Council for British Archaeology and with the help of other official interested organisations, he embarked on the near impossible task of travelling over the whole Roman road system in Britain, and in so doing covered 20,000 miles (30,000 km), invariably in an immaculate Austin car of ancient vintage. Thus were published by Phoenix House in 1955 Volume I and in 1957 Volume II of his great work. Once the first volume was published it inspired many who read it to attempt the filling in of missing road gaps, which some did with great success, using his methods. He had devised a system of road numbering, single figures for important roads, double for secondary roads and three figures for minor roads. Now that he was the leading authority an amusing etiquette developed between him and his correspondents. If you believed you had discovered an unknown Roman road, you carefully collected all the facts and photographs and submitted them to him, the word 'Roman' being omitted if possible, 'ancient' or 'old' being used instead. Then, if you were lucky, he would say, 'Your route may be worthy of inclusion', and later, almost as an afterthought, he would give it the next appropriate number. This was not done lightly or before a personal visit to the sites where the best parts existed. So it was that a Margary Roman road number became the highest honour one's research work could receive, personal and unique. It is a matter of great regret that there will be no further Margary numbers issued, no more correspondence or encouragement from him, or endorsement of any sort. A one-volume edition of *Roman Roads in Britain* was published by John Baker in 1967.

A meticulous work on the detection of roads in a selected area, called *Roman Roads in the South-East Midlands,* was written by an experienced group calling themselves the Viatores (meaning 'travellers' in Latin) and published by Victor Gollancz Ltd in 1964. (It is now out of print and obtainable only on the second-hand market and on loan from libraries.) Margary's book is currently the standard work on the subject in Britain, and the reader is recommended to obtain a copy.

There are two other types of person who have been involved in the discovery of Roman roads. The first is the professional archaeologist. The subject of Roman roads is not normally taught at university level and is incidental to the study of Roman Britain. Even I. D. Margary made no endowment for further research. The experienced amateur need not, therefore, feel at a disadvantage when faced with a professional, but he must expect a cautious attitude from the latter on account of his scientific training. Sometimes this does go too far and amounts to a failure to face facts. Differences of opinion are one thing but drawing wrong conclusions as a result of bias against the amateur is quite inexcusable. Both make genuine mistakes and we must spot these, go back to established facts and original sources, form our own opinions and be ready to modify them if necessary.

One of the most famous professionals of recent years was Sir Mortimer Wheeler, and his axiom that Roman roads were just a part of the whole picture of Roman Britain cannot be faulted. He excavated *Verulamium* in the early 1930s with Mrs T. V. Wheeler and dealt fairly and fully with Watling Street in his report of 1936, the index listing twenty-five mentions, but listed under 'Roads' there is nothing, and under 'Roadways' only one mention. In other words, he did not discuss what he was unfamiliar with at first hand. Because he did not mention any roads besides Watling Street it does not follow that none existed, and he was aware of the roads to Silchester and Colchester that ran from the city gates. We are certain from later research by R. H. Reid and C. Morris that there were at least a dozen roads out of the city (fig. 1). The lesson is obvious. It is worth looking again at all the towns in Roman Britain (particularly those with 'chester' in the name) to ascertain if there is further work to be done, and if so to do it. It is unlikely that professional archaeologists will have already dealt with the problems adequately.

The second type of involvement is that of the aerial photographer; the end product is either high or low level vertical photographs, or low level oblique pictures. Unknown sites may be observed on these, if the photographs were taken near dawn or sunset, by the casting of shadows from surface irregularities, and more importantly by crop marks, which need a word of explanation and a reference to fig. 2. Here the condition, density and colour of arable crops indicate what lies below without need for excavation. A crop grows best over a ditch and worst over a buried wall or road. The finest conditions are obtainable in June with a crop of barley. In times of drought the effect may also be seen in grass on pasture land. Crop marks cannot be expected to reveal Roman roads under hedgerows or modern roads.

Among the pioneers of aerial photography were the late Major G. W. G. Allen and O. G. S. Crawford, who were active before the Second World War (Allen's negatives are in the Ashmolean Museum, Oxford), and since then Professor J. K. St Joseph of Cambridge University has had much success in discovering hundreds of unknown Romano-British sites.

One of the largest collections in Britain, which may be viewed on application, is held by the National Monuments Record, Fortress House, 23 Savile Row, London W1X 1AD.

Aerofilms Limited, a division of Hunting Surveys and Consultants Limited, can supply oblique and vertical aerial photographs of almost any subject in the British Isles to order or from negatives held at their library at Boreham Wood.

In recent years, notably in the dry summers of 1975, 1976 and 1989, archaeological organisations big and small seized the opportunity to photograph from the air a multitude of previously unknown sites, and the results have still to be fully evaluated.

Even so, aerial photographs are very useful but not essential for the discovery of Roman roads. There is much to be seen on the ground but it might take longer. Indeed, some features are noticeable only on the ground and not from the air, so a conjunction of both methods is indicated.

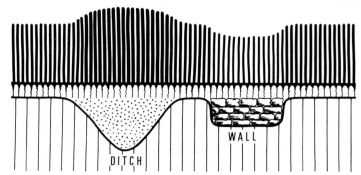

Fig. 2. An explanation of crop markings. A Roman road would produce the same effect as the wall shown.

Fig. 3. A cross-section through an average Roman road showing the *agger* or embankment, metalling, side and outer ditches.

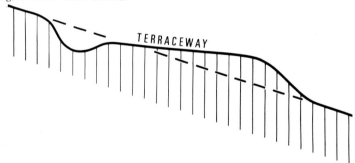

Fig. 4. A cross-section through a typical Roman terraceway on a hillside.

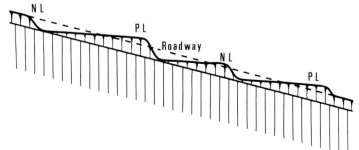

Fig. 5. A cross-section through a double lynchet way. NL = negative lynchet. PL = positive lynchet.

2
Roman road construction

Roman roads linked Roman sites which were invariably situated near a water supply and often a day's march apart, that is 10 to 15 miles (16 to 24 km). The sites could be initially Claudian forts, posting stations (*mansiones* in Latin) rather like the cavalry forts of the American west, developed towns or tribal capitals. Road intersections did not always occur at the centre of such sites but sometimes outside their walls. It is possible that the intention was to provide a road grid of squares whose sides were about 12 miles (19 km) with occupied sites at the nodal points over the whole province, as well as radial roads from major towns and cities. This is clearly an over-simplification, for the plan was modified and never fully achieved. It would be very easy if one could take all the known sites and join each to the other with straight lines, but that was not quite the way it happened. Unless an ancient road joins two Roman sites and bears somewhere along it clear evidence of the characteristic raised appearance of the Roman causeway or *agger*, perhaps only for a short distance, then on surface evidence the road cannot qualify as Roman in origin.

In most cases road alignments were laid out by the surveyors from one hilltop to another. These sighting points would be mutually visible, possibly with the aid of fires and beacons. Intermediate points on the same line could be laid out easily on lower ground, not necessarily dead straight as more useful purposes could sometimes be served by slight deviations to avoid natural obstacles, or even man-made ones like burial mounds. To descend escarpments or cross rivers it was permissible to zigzag and dig terraceways or make cuttings as required by the nature of the locality rather than stick to the rigid straight line. Steep gradients up to 1 in 6 and fording of rivers were not deterrents. Indeed bridges were vulnerable and only seem to have been provided where there was no practicable alternative. Crossing of marshes was achieved by first placing a foundation of brushwood under the road proper, and one case is known in the Fens where the porous subsoil was replaced to a considerable depth by another of finer particle size to hold back flooding.

Thus any suggestion that all Roman roads were dead straight from one place to another, mile after mile, is just not true and presupposes that the surveyors had no intelligence or common sense and blindly followed the rule book regardless of terrain.

On the contrary, Roman surveyors in Britain displayed the highest skills in laying out roads in the most sensible manner without either following slavishly the direct line or departing too far from it. In this work they had much the same problems as the more recent railway surveyors in choosing the best route between two places and it is noteworthy that where the problem was the same the two solutions were not very far apart. Between Bedford and Wellingborough, south of which town there was also a Roman one at Irchester on the river Nene, the problem was one of crossing the winding river Ouse at the minimum number of places. The Romans did this at three places and the railway engineers managed it in no less than seven. Some other considerations of the Roman surveyor's ability show that this was little short of miraculous. A well-known instance is the line of Stane Street as laid out between Chichester and London. In no way on the ground then or now could one place be seen from the other. Yet from Old London Bridge as far as Ewell the alignment was directed at Chichester's east gate; the geology of the district was taken into account to create nine alignments, three of them major, the whole in modern surveying terms being a 'closed traverse'. Nobody knows how it was done.

No planning applications were required in those days, so work could be begun without delay, but much organisation was needed to transport materials, tools and labour and to feed and shelter the labourers. They could not have been slaves under subjugation dying in their hundreds by the wayside because only occasionally is the unfortunate Roman, with a coin in his mouth to see him across the river Styx, disturbed accidentally during ditch clearing.

When today we talk of ridgeways, the Icknield Way and Roman roads under the general term of ancient lines of communication it is well to appreciate that the Icknield Way, being of probable neolithic origin, was to the Romans about 2,500 years old and the ridgeways considerably older than that. Therefore, they would have been in dire need of repair. Notwithstanding this, it would have been apparent to the Roman that where they would serve a useful purpose they could be restored, metalled in many cases and brought up to standard, although they would not have been accurately aligned in the first place. Considering the desire to keep their roads on high ground as far as practicable, it is not surprising that many ridgeways, neolithic routes and iron-age trackways were pressed into service perhaps late in the first century AD and Romanised. There were no doubt exceptions in that certain pre-existing routes — the Akeman Street and Watling Street for instance — were given the full treatment straight away, the evidence being that the Akeman Street, if thought of as the route from London to Bath, curves round the north of the Thames valley and duplicates a more obviously Roman road via Silchester and Speen, and the Watling Street not only links Belgic cities (Canterbury and St Albans) but misses Roman London altogether at the Thames crossing (Westminster Bridge).

Leaving these aside, imagine flat, wooded, virgin territory between two hilltop sighting points, requiring a straight 30 feet (9m) wide roadway to be constructed upon it.

Firstly, the woodland would have to be cleared by chopping down and burning to a width of at least 90 feet (27m). Then parallel outer ditches would be ploughed, say 90 feet (27m) apart, at the edges of the clearing. Thus would the road zone be defined and marked out initially. Then the same plough would mark out the road proper in the centre of the zone perhaps by ditches 30 feet (27m) apart, though this could vary from 15 feet to 50 feet (5 to 15m). An embankment would be built up between the two centre ditches using material from a scoop-ditch, leaving a wide depression along one or both sides of the road, which later traffic might travel along and wear deeper into a hollow way. On top of that a foundation of local large stones would be laid, followed by smaller stones, flints or gravel, well cambered to give good drainage, called the 'road metal' or 'metalling', not an ideal term except possibly in the one instance where iron slag was used, at Holtye in East Sussex. The road embankment used to be referred to as the 'causeway' by earlier archaeologists but now it is universally described by the Latin name *agger*. Covered with later topsoil it appears as a hump varying from a few inches in height to several feet. Together with dykes, ditches and boundary banks it comes under the general classification of 'linear earthworks' (fig. 3).

This hump or *agger* running along the side of a hill or slope may be described as a 'hillside *agger*' to distinguish it from a normal Roman terraceway, with uphill ditch, roadway sloping outwards of width from about 10 feet to 25 feet (3 to 8m), sometimes metalled, very often not, especially on chalk subsoil (fig. 4.). To complicate matters further there is the 'double lynchet way' (fig. 5) associated with farming Celtic fields, not necessarily a piece of Roman civil engineering but formed by ploughing along the contours in one direction only over a long period of time. It can be included as part of the chain of evidence sought for in establishing the line of a previously unknown stretch of Roman road.

Though not very common, cuttings were made through the tops of hills to ease the gradients but seem to have been confined to the earlier military roads.

The procedure for crossing a river was usually quite simple. The preference was for fords in large numbers and no doubt during the course of marching there were many wet feet, and more besides if the water came up to the waist. Fords were of two types: paved with stones held with mortar and piles, with steps leading down to the river and out again; and simple types of natural form or perhaps a tongue of gravel to consolidate the river bottom. Paved fords are very rare; only three so far are known in Britain (fig. 6, plates 30 and 45).

Bridges would be called for where the riverbanks and depths precluded fords. Until recently not much was known about bridges in Britain except that they must have been simply constructed of wood, probably oak, though elm is a possibility. The finest masonry bridges are to be found on the continent; those in Rome are most impressive, notably the Pons Aemilius and the lower half of the Pons Aelius leading over the river Tiber to the tomb of Hadrian (now the Castel Sant' Angelo). The Pons Milvius and Pons Nomentana were of massive construction.

Those known in Britain were much smaller. The most celebrated in southern England is that formerly at Alfoldean, West Sussex, which was fully documented by the late S. E. Winbolt. Here the Stane Street, after passing through the posting station on the south bank, crosses the river Arun slightly to the east of the modern road A29. Oak piles were first noticed by him when the river level was low in 1934 and were subsequently recovered, together with squared stones and Roman tiles, and a plan of the site was drawn (fig. 6 and plate 12). Nothing of interest remains there now, but it would be useful if divers could investigate similar sites and add to the sparse knowledge of these structures. One place which has always been intriguing is the spot where the Ermine Street crossed the river Nene west of Peterborough. This can be located with precision but nothing can be seen from boats or banks.

A recent excavation of a bridge at Aldwincle, Northamptonshire, was carried out by T. M. Ambrose and D. Jackson and was published in *Britannia* for 1976. In the article they discussed the types of Roman timber bridge found in the province.

There are some places where there must have been Roman ferry services. One example is across the mouth of the Wash from Holme-next-the-Sea, adjacent to Hunstanton, Norfolk, where the Peddars Way ends abruptly. On the opposite shore another Roman road leads from Lincoln right to the coast just south of Skegness. Such a route from Norfolk to Lincoln would save a considerable distance crossing the Fenlands.

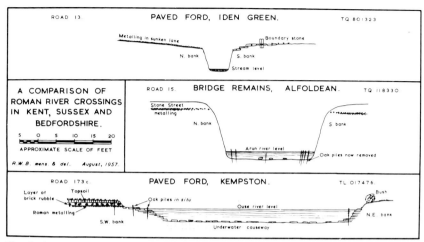

Fig. 6. A comparison of Roman river crossings.

Another possible ferry service might have been across the Solent between Stone Point and a point west of Cowes on the Isle of Wight (*Vectis* to the Romans), the whole of which awaits investigation by a field worker.

It has been stated that Roman milestones were placed at mile intervals along the roads. If this were so, then one could expect a total of about ten thousand placed. Recent research by J. P. Sedgley gives a tally of 110. This represents 1.1 per cent of the possible total so far recovered or recorded. From the writer's experience over about 400 miles (650 km) of tracing Roman roads no milestones at all were found, only a mulling stone for grinding corn, fortunately probably unique (plate 55), and this was not for lack of trying. However, the inscriptions are of little help, being eulogies of reigning emperors; the mileage between places is often omitted or illegible (plate 54).

3
Contemporary maps and other documentary evidence

Unlike the roads radiating out of Rome, which were given names as described earlier, Roman roads in Britain were not so distinguished and there is no way of telling how they were labelled. Names were first given by the Anglo-Saxons, who referred to Roman roads as *streats* from the metalled layer on the surface. Thus, where place-names of early origin occur, such as Chester-le-Street, Markyate Street, Streatham, Streatley, Stratton, Stretton and variations of these, one can nearly always be certain of the proximity of a Roman road. Equally, *Stan, Stone* and *-ford* names are worth a closer look. So too are Ridgeways and Causeways which are not bridge approaches. For some unknown reason, unconnected Roman roads sometimes bear the same name, as for instance Watling Street, Akeman Street, Ermine Street, and there are several Port Ways. The Welsh Roman road is often referred to as Sarn Helen. Sometimes a road is simply called Roman Road. Names of apparently Latin origin, such as *Via Devana* and *Via Julia,* are comparatively modern inventions.

In about AD 210 there appeared the *Itinerary of Antoninus,* which was a road book attributed to Caracalla (M. Aurelius Antoninus). It gives lists of towns and other places with distances in Roman miles between them. It has taken some years to equate the information of the itineraries with archaeological evidence but a picture has been built up fixing the ancient Roman names in the correct places on the principal roads with a great degree of certainty.

One cannot expect documents of such age to survive in their original form, so as they became damaged and faded they would be copied and copied again. There is in existence a thirteenth-century copy of a third-century road map which was discovered in the library of Conrad Peutinger of Augsburg and goes by the name of *Tabula Peutingeriana.* It is a series of parchment strips rolled up. Since Britain was mostly on the outer strip, which was lost together with the information on it, only a small south-eastern portion of the island on the next sheet survived and this proved to be inaccurate.

There was also the seventh-century Ravenna Cosmography, similar in some ways to the Antonine Itineraries with its lists of place-names in corrupt forms, but those who have examined it advise that not too much importance should be attached to it.

Moving on a little in time, one should mention the thirteenth-century map of the monk Matthew Paris of St Albans, and the fourteenth-century Gough Map in the Bodleian Library at Oxford, which is fairly useful and accurate so far as England is concerned. Copies of these maps are not difficult to obtain.

There may possibly have been instances where in monastic times monks not only kept roads and bridges in repair but also constructed new ones. I. D. Margary once or twice talked of raised causeways of monastic origin, but what evidence there may have been for this is not known to the writer. So far as the county of Bedfordshire is concerned, there is no evidence whatever of medieval roads being constructed.

It is fairly safe to assume, therefore, that between the time the Romans left Britain in AD 410 and the date of the first turnpike act in 1663, which covered the Great North Road between Stilton, Cambridgeshire, and Wadesmill, Hertfordshire, no engineered roads were constructed. Any roads that came into existence between these dates happened naturally and would have been winding and unmetalled.

This is of considerable help to us in tracing Roman roads by a process of elimination, but there is also another useful factor to consider. This was that parish and county boundaries were first laid down between the eighth and tenth centuries AD, and what better features to mark them were there than rivers, old trackways and Roman roads? Since about 1900 AD there have been further changes in the siting of parish and county boundaries, but if one uses earlier Ordnance Survey maps it nearly always follows that where a parish or county boundary coincides with a trackway, green lane, footpath or road, then these are very old and it is simply a question then of looking for the hand of the Roman road builder in their construction, or deciding that they are too haphazard to be attributable to the Romans.

In the middle of the eighteenth century William Stukeley was the leading antiquary. In 1747 he received a letter from Charles Julius Bertram, then aged twenty-four, whose father was a silk dyer in London. Bertram had been living in Copenhagen, Denmark, for four years and taught English at the Marine Academy there. A correspondence between them developed and eventually Bertram mentioned he had seen an account in a friend's possession of a history of Roman Britain together with a map of the same purporting to have been compiled by a monk called Richard of Westminster. Stukeley persuaded Bertram to copy both Latin text and map and send it to him, which was done piecemeal. He then advised Bertram to publish the work, which was carried out in

Copenhagen in 1757 in the first instance, together with histories from two other monks. Stukeley found out that a Richard of Cirencester had lived at Westminster Abbey at one time, so that the book was published as *Britannicarum Gentium Historiae Antiquae Scriptores Tres: Ricardus Corinensis, Gildas Badonicus, Nennius Banchorensis* and due credit was claimed by the editor, 'Carolus Bertramus' for his part. The portion by Richard of Cirencester was called *De Situ Britanniae* and consisted of forty-eight pages of Latin, in the form of an expanded Antonine Itinerary, and the map which, to translate the inscription at the foot, was 'drawn and engraved from the original by C. Bertram himself' (plate 27). It was hailed at the time as an important addition to literature and knowledge.

Both Stukeley and Bertram died in 1765. Then, after some dissension from 1827 onwards, they were severely criticised between 1866 and 1869 by B. B. Woodward and J. E. B. Mayor, one for being a forger and the other for being taken in by it. The present writer has not seen the copies of the *Gentleman's Magazine* where the main exposure was made but has read a later version by H. J. Randall entitled *'Splendide Mendax'* printed in *Antiquity* for March 1933, where further denigration occurs, most of it very convincing. The *Dictionary of National Biography* in the meantime has already described Bertram as 'the cleverest and most successful literary impostor of modern times' and the Ordnance Survey has busied itself removing the *De Situ* place-names off its maps.

But having looked up the facts for the purposes of this book, and knowing that very experienced (now deceased) colleagues treated the matter as an elaborate joke in poor taste, the present writer is still puzzled why a man should have been persuaded to sit down for many hours in a foreign country, invent and write forty-eight pages of fictional Latin and fabricate a complicated map, all for little monetary gain. If he had wanted notoriety, he could have done it a lot more easily and with less risk of being found out by Stukeley. Some of the mistakes could be explained away by ambiguities, errors of copying or misunderstandings. The missing original map could have been fragile and torn up as of no further use.

Most worrying of all, some aspects of *De Situ* appear to have been prophetic. Was this luck or, as Randall suggested, highly intelligent and cunning research?

Perhaps this diversion may illustrate how necessary it is in studying the subject not to believe everything said or written but instead to go back if possible to the original historical source or the evidence of one's own eyes before coming to any decision or expressed opinion.

4
Roman roads in decline and later roads

The Roman army was recalled from Britain by AD 410 after nearly four hundred years, by which time many generations had become used to their presence and considerable intermingling of ethnic groups had taken place. Indeed, there could not have been many persons of purely Roman or British origin left. Thus the country passed into the dark ages and there was a period of chaos and uncertainty, lack of records for the historian and generally very thin unrevealing layers for the archaeologist to interpret.

During that period the roads fell into disuse and were not repaired, but probably the bridges would have been the first to go, perhaps not too serious a problem with all the fording places still intact. Trees and other obstacles which fell across the line were not removed; wayfarers would have simply walked round them. Hollow ways and traffic ruts were formed and became deeper as time went on. Roads, like old wood, became warped and off-centre in the road zone.

With the arrival of the Anglo-Saxons and other invaders from the continent Roman buildings were sometimes deliberately destroyed and signs of panic are evidenced by the occasional discovery of coin and other hoards which were never claimed and became treasure trove.

In this period, as already stated, place-names developed such as *straet* and derivatives. One other, *Coldharbour* and its associate *Caldecot,* meaning 'cold shelter or cottage' or 'shelter from the cold' (*cf* sunshade) has a definite connection with Roman roads. What exactly they looked like is not known, and observed excavations reveal nothing, suggesting they were organic and destructible. Possibly they were tents of some sort. It used to be tactless to mention the connection in knowledgeable circles, especially as it was only an opinion. However, it is now respectable as the matter was tackled by T. R. Ogden at Durham University in 1966, using statistical analysis and a computer, and he found in favour of the association.

Another place-name puzzle which deserves similar treatment is still only a theory and a hunch and it is this: if we eliminate Follies meaning architectural foolishness and those meaning leafy bowers (foliage) we are left with others which make no sense but which occur with uncomfortable frequency along Roman roads. Possibly they were something to do with the verb *to follow*. We do not know the answer, but it will pay us to keep an eye open for them. Examples are Folly Farm, Folly Lane and so on.

The English Place-Name Society has since 1926 been producing surveys county by county, the first being a joint volume on Bedfordshire and Huntingdonshire. They are essential for study, especially as they include field names. Not all counties have been treated so far. The publishers are Cambridge University Press and copies are available in local reference libraries, as are Victoria County Histories, the Romano-British sections of which should also be consulted.

After the dark ages, there came a period in the middle ages when parishioners were made responsible for the upkeep of the highways in their own parishes. They often defaulted and were indicted for neglect of their duty.

At one time it was commonplace to rob the road of its metalling for some other purpose such as wall building or filling in potholes. Most flagrant of all was to build a house, or even a church or chapel, right on top of the *agger*, using it as a foundation. In such cases the secret is to look not at the ground but at the roof, to observe the tell-tale curvature (plate 43).

The berms on each side of the *agger* eventually became wide roadside verges; but on occasion, because they appeared to belong to nobody in particular, astute cottage owners either cultivated the patch or put the whole cottage on it as well. These are known, not surprisingly, as encroachments.

Because Roman roads are often to be found underneath hedgerows, a theory suggests itself that following disuse, weed seeds became lodged in between the stones and a hedge would be self-sown. The writer knows of a case where a fence was erected and a sizable hedge appeared as well after twenty years or so, without any help from man.

The act compelling parishioners to repair and maintain the highways was passed in 1555 and the present writer listed all the cases in the Quarter Sessions Rolls for Bedfordshire between 1714 and 1832 (which were readily available reprinted from the original records) in which the words 'ancient highway' were mentioned.

Some possible Roman roads were discovered in this way but the overall result was disappointing. Perhaps for different counties other researchers may be more fortunate. County record offices are mines of information and their staff are always most helpful.

5
Tracing unknown Roman roads

The following advice on how to go about tracing and discovering unknown Roman roads is based on the work of I. D. Margary and, to a lesser extent, R. H. Reid and others whose writings are noted in the bibliography. These methods have withstood the test of time and can almost be guaranteed to give good results to any intelligent person with reasonable powers of observation.

Ordnance Survey (OS) maps are essential, being the only ones sufficiently accurate for our purposes. Because of metrication the old one-inch and six-inch scales are being phased out and instead one has to buy 1:50,000 and 1:10,000 scales. These seem to lack the exemplary hand-produced result of the earlier maps, which had considerable merit and character, so the reader is urged to obtain second-hand whatever maps he can at any scale covering the area he wishes to explore. Parish boundaries may well have been changed on the new maps, so it is as well to go back fifty or a hundred years to find the situation as it was.

David and Charles, in conjunction with the Ordnance Survey, have covered the whole of the British Isles with a series of reprints of the first edition of the one-inch OS map, and these are most useful for the information they contain about many means of communication.

Geological maps will have to be consulted occasionally, but this is best done at the local library. There you will also find facilities for photocopying. Care should be taken not to infringe the Copyright, Designs and Patents Act of 1988, but usually there is no objection to single copies being made for the purpose of research.

Please remember also that if you venture on to private property it is necessary to obtain the owner's permission first to avoid trespass, but most of the time you will be on publicly owned property, roads, National Trust land, parks, bridleways and footpaths. It is a good idea to keep to these as far as practicable.

The first job is to take the OS outline map of the area to be explored, whether it be to the scale of 1 inch to 1 mile or 1:50,000, and go over it square by square. Underline in red waterproof ink or pencil all the *streat, Coldharbour, Caldecot, Chester* place-names, and put a query against *Folly, stone, -ford, ridgeway* and *causeway* names.

Mark on all Roman information, some of which may already be there, in which case it should be accentuated. Refer to the latest edition of the

OS *Map of Roman Britain* (currently this is the third edition of 1956,
which is rather out of date) to double-check that nothing has been missed.
The same symbols and abbreviations that the Ordnance Survey uses can
be picked out in red on the outline map for villas, milestones, etc. Coins
and odd potsherds are not important and can be omitted. Roman burials
are important, because it was the custom to site cemeteries beside roads
and outside town walls. Add all the other road information from previous
sources mentioned, notably I. D. Margary's 1967 book. It is best to do this
in pencil, in case mistakes are made. When this is done, carry out the
same work, square by square, on the six-inch or 1:10,000 scale maps. If
something of interest is marked which is not on the first map, it can be
added now. It may be desirable to join two maps of the same scale
together for continuity and this must be done accurately with adhesive
which will not wrinkle the paper.

Now it will become apparent that there are many gaps in our knowledge
of Roman roads. Some known ones seem to end suddenly for no obvious
reason. Others have large missing portions but continue after perhaps a
mile or two at some distant place, maybe on a different alignment. A road
which enters a Roman town from, say, the west, nearly always goes out
again on the east side. Try to ascertain by studying the maps where
discontinued roads may have been making for, that is, a Roman site on
the projected line. See if the changes of alignment can be spotted on
hilltops or at fords and bridges. Join up known portions where there are
gaps (lightly in pencil) to form a base line along which to search for
missing remains, and put a query against straight roads, paths and
hedgerows which carry parish or county boundaries.

Next make a quick preliminary reconnaissance in a car, preferably
driven by someone else for reasons of safety, along the whole route end to

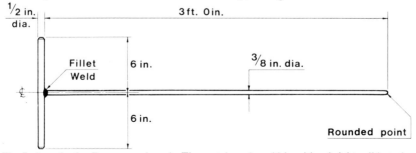

Fig. 7. A probe for Roman road work. The metal used could be either bright mild steel or
stainless steel. For heavy persons the diameters should be increased to ⅝ inch and ½ inch
respectively.

end, noting the appearance of known portions of the road, the general nature of the terrain and any obvious signs of the *agger*. This is best done in the winter when hedges and trees are leafless and the lie of the land is most visible. It can also be carried out on horseback (as they used to), bicycle, train, or helicopter if you have one.

Next, the field worker must examine the ground minutely along the base line and each side of it. This is done by walking along the line away from the car and back again so that it is observed from at least two directions.

Take the six-inch maps, cameras, polythene bags, food, plastic mackintosh, wellingtons and anything else that might be needed for a hike of several miles. A probe made of two pieces of mild steel (fig. 7) is useful if you want to feel the Roman surface metalling below the present topsoil, but do not attempt this in places where it might upset a farmer, cause suspicion or where there might be unexploded bombs or shells from the Second World War.

Notes must be made in pencil on the maps of features observed as you progress, and these need not be elaborate. The following abbreviations have been helpful to others in the past:

AA	alignment angle	GL	green lane
Agger	(in full)	HR	hedgerow on line
AP	air photograph	HSA	hillside agger
BR	bridle road on line	HW	hollow way
CB	county boundary	MR	modern road on line
CTG	cutting	MV	metalling visible
CW	causeway	PB	parish boundary
DLW	double lynchet way	R	Roman
DR	derelict road	R-B	Romano-British
E	encroachment	R & FP	ridge and furrow
EIA	early iron age		ploughing
EW	edge of wood on line	SECT	section
FB	field boundary	SD	side ditch
	other than hedge	TW	terraceway
FP	footpath on line	WV	wide verge

Even if you only find one short length of *agger* in 5 or even 10 miles (8 to 16 km) of searching, the mission will have been successful. Experience has shown that there is no need to be as pessimistic as this, however.

The process is very often a matter of correcting previous work done by others, but it is not unusual to find mistakes and one need not lose faith in our predecessors. One or two corrections do not invalidate the whole line of a Roman road.

Sometimes the appearance of the *agger* is very subtle, and obvious humps may represent the remains of park banks, infilling of pipe trenches, early iron-age territorial boundaries, disused railway embankments and so on. It is, therefore, advisable to cut a section across the suspect *agger,* after first obtaining any necessary permission.

Inexperienced excavators cannot ruin a dig for a Roman road, unlike many other types of site, where each is unique. It is a useful training ground for novices, who must first be persuaded that a stony layer is the target, and nothing more romantic than that.

Sections

About 20 tons (2000 kg) of material has to be removed and replaced for each section attempted. For this, one needs intelligent volunteer labour and these persons have to be insured against possible injury.

For tools one needs pickaxes (though only experts should use them), forks, shovels of the heart-shaped kind, brushes, pointing trowels, surveying, marking out and recording equipment. Grass, if on pasture land, should be cut first, turves removed and piled neatly well clear of operations.

The trench is marked out 1 yard (or 1 metre) wide at right angles to the road's line, and a start is made digging out topsoil in the centre of the hump and working from there outwards to include the two side ditches if present. Spoil (excavated material) should be thrown well clear of the trench in a direction away from the sun (for photographic purposes) and the sides kept neat and vertical. The first objective is to expose the top metalled surface, which may be medieval or later, work down to the Roman layers, photograph each stage with ranging rods as scales and break through to the natural subsoil. Then a cross-section of the road should be drawn at a scale of say ½ inch to 1 foot on squared paper using a builder's line as a horizontal datum and plotting vertical co-ordinates from it at regular intervals. A suggested key to sections is printed here as fig. 8.

The site should always be returned to its former condition and left as tidy as possible to avoid complaints.

The excavators only act under law as the agents of the landowner and any finds are the latter's property, unless they happen to be of gold or silver, when a coroner's inquest must be held.

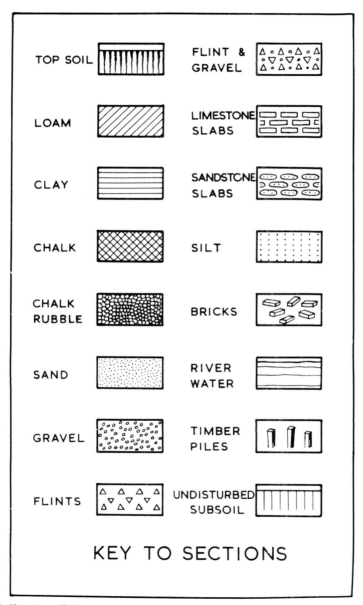

Fig. 8. Key to sections.

6
Photographic recording

Travelling on foot means carrying lightweight equipment; I carry two cameras, one for 120 film black and white ASA 400 (actually Ilford HP5) and one for 35 mm colour transparencies (Agfa Chrome CT100, which reproduces greens well). For colour prints Fujicolor Super HR100 is satisfactory. Both cameras are rangefinder type and of maximum aperture f/3.5. Do not buy lenses of larger aperture, twin lens reflex cameras or single lens reflex cameras with interchangeable lenses, if you wish to avoid carrying around a large amount of useless glass. A light meter is important and I use a Weston Mk V, which seems capable of taking the occasional mishap.

Colour transparencies are sent to the manufacturers' processing divisions, who usually give good service. If one is careful in loading, it is possible to obtain one or two more slides per spool. It is advisable to make the first exposure of an unimportant subject, one's name and address or car registration number so that it can be traced to the owner.

Black and white negatives to be processed by oneself are developed by the time/temperature method in fine grain developer such as Kodak D76 or Ilford ID11. The spiral is loaded in pitch darkness, and the rest carried out in normal light. The negatives when fixed are washed for at least an hour in filtered water, dried, numbered and filed.

Two prints are made from each negative to En-print size, which is somewhere between postcard size and quarter-plate. At the moment of exposure or soon afterwards a note must be made and taken from the map of the grid reference number, indicating the position of the camera and the direction towards which it was pointing. This and other particulars of subject, parish, date and negative should be entered on the back of each print in soft pencil. One copy will be filed in chronological order and the other mounted on loose-leaf sheets under respective parishes in alphabetical order.

If possible, include unobtrusively some indication of scale such as human figures or cars, or, if of purely archaeological interest, surveyors' ranging rods placed vertically in the centre of each side ditch.

No useful purpose is served by recording exposure times and 'f' numbers. A 2X yellow filter may be used to increase contrast.

Finally the negative numbers and date taken should be entered in the margins of the field maps for possible future reference.

7
Publication

Publication of one's work is among the most difficult tasks one has to perform in connection with Roman roads and there is no short cut. There is an obligation on the part of a researcher to disseminate his or her results. There is no such obligation on book publishers to risk their money on something which stands no chance of being a bestseller, but some accept possible losses for prestige purposes.

Normally one would write up an account of a newly discovered road as an article for a county archaeological journal or, if the road runs through a number of counties, one might consider one of the national journals like *Britannia* or the *Archaeological Journal*. Advice on where to publish can usually be obtained from your local museum or archaeological society, which would appreciate copies of your maps and field notes when you have finished with them.

Grants to assist publication can be obtained from philanthropic sources. You must accept that you will most likely not be paid for your effort and expense but will receive a great deal of enjoyment in its place. It will be necessary to have a duplicated report of the fieldwork and other research to hawk around, so this should be tackled as soon as possible, keeping to facts and avoiding speculation. Eventually patience and persistence should achieve the desired result.

8
Recommended sites

Probably the most important British road to the Romans was Watling Street, which ran from Dover to Wroxeter (Margary 1a to 1h). It is possible to follow the major part from end to end by using the modern roads A2, A5, etc, but one can examine the road in its original state only at selected places such as the gates of *Verulamium* (St Albans), between Redbourn and Dunstable, where there are divergences, and similar places. It is not a good road for inspection.

Ermine Street (2a to 2e) is rather better since the characteristic large *agger* can be appreciated as it passes through *Durobrivae* (Water Newton) as a large hump in the arable field, and beyond northwards through Normangate Field, Castor, on to the area south-east of Stamford, all, please note, on private land.

Akeman Street (16a and 16b), the Foss Way (5a to 5f) and Peddars Way (33a and 33b) are largely superseded by modern roads superimposed on the old line and are easily followed by car.

The Romanised Icknield Way (168a and 168b) is very suitable for foot travel but consists mainly of continuous unmetalled green lanes rather untypical of Roman construction, because it was a minor Roman road mostly on chalk, which offered good drainage and only required a turved surface.

I. D. Margary, whose experience was without equal, would possibly have recommended a visit to Ackling Dyke (4c) in Wiltshire and Dorset, where he described the *agger* between Old Sarum and Badbury Rings as magnificent, up to 50 feet (15 m) wide and 6 feet (1.8 m) high.

In the south-east midlands unquestionably the finest length is to be seen in Claypits Field, Warden Street, Bedfordshire (plates 32 and 33). This must be viewed from the road since it is on farmed pasture land and privately owned.

Here and there, throughout the United Kingdom, deliberately preserved portions exist such as the iron slag road at Holtye, East Sussex (14), the paved road in the Forest of Dean at Blackpool Bridge (614) and the paved road at Blackstone Edge, Greater Manchester (720a; plate 49).

The best Roman road on which to learn the techniques of tracing and discovery would probably be the Stane Street (15) in West Sussex and Surrey, because so much fieldwork and excavation has been carried out on it in the past, published in numerous articles and several books (listed in the select bibliography). Therefore one's own suppositions and theories can be checked and corrected if necessary by a visit to the local reference library. The present writer learned much this way.

To avoid much travel and possible disappointment, the reader should begin by studying closely the known Roman roads in his own vicinity and thus establish whether or not he wishes to pursue the subject further.

9
Select bibliography

General

Chevalier, Raymond. *Roman Roads*. Batsford, 1976. Revised paperback edition 1989. Includes continental roads.

Margary, I. D. *Roman Roads in Britain*. John Baker, 1967. The definitive work on the subject and essential reading.

Johnston, D. E. *An Illustrated History of Roman Roads in Britain*. Spurbooks, 1979. Part theoretical, part topographical.

Maps

Webster, Graham. *Roman Britain*. Observer Maps, George Philip and Son, 1976. Good but understandably incomplete.

Ordnance Survey. *Map of Roman Britain* (4th edition, 1978).

Regional

Margary, I. D. *Roman Ways in the Weald*. Phoenix House, 1949.

Viatores, The. *Roman Roads in the South-East Midlands*. Victor Gollancz, 1964.

Reid, R. H. 'Tracing Roman Roads', *The Amateur Historian,* vol. 4, no. 7 (1960) 282-90.

Individual

Thomas, Edward. *The Icknield Way*. Constable, 1913.

Belloc, Hilaire. *The Stane Street*. Constable, 1913.

Grant, W. A. *The Topography of Stane Street*. John Long, 1922.

Winbolt, S. E. *With a Spade on Stane Street*. Methuen, 1936.

Berry, Bernard. *A Lost Roman Road*. George Allen & Unwin, 1963.

Bagshawe, R. W. and T. W. 'An Early Antiquary and his Friends', *Bedfordshire Magazine,* vol. 9, no. 66 (1963) 57-60. Thomas Leman, William Bennet, Charles Mason and Thomas Pownall.

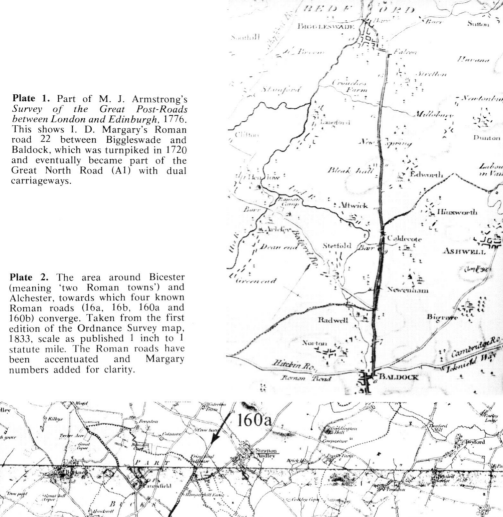

Plate 1. Part of M. J. Armstrong's *Survey of the Great Post-Roads between London and Edinburgh*, 1776. This shows I. D. Margary's Roman road 22 between Biggleswade and Baldock, which was turnpiked in 1720 and eventually became part of the Great North Road (A1) with dual carriageways.

Plate 2. The area around Bicester (meaning 'two Roman towns') and Alchester, towards which four known Roman roads (16a, 16b, 160a and 160b) converge. Taken from the first edition of the Ordnance Survey map, 1833, scale as published 1 inch to 1 statute mile. The Roman roads have been accentuated and Margary numbers added for clarity.

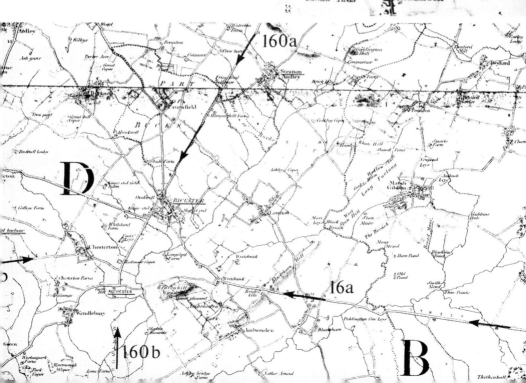

Plate 3. Oblique aerial photograph looking north-west towards Great Brickhill, Bucks, showing the modern trunk road A5 coincident with Watling Street (1e). In the foreground is the Fox and Hounds public house at the fork leading to Woburn along the A418. (Copyright: Aerofilms Ltd.)

Plate 4. Watling Street (1e) represented by the A5 modern road at Stony Stratford, Bucks, a place-name that has three elements indicating the presence of a Roman road. (Copyright: Aerofilms Ltd.)

Plate 5. Watling Street (1e) at Hockliffe, Beds, coincident with the A5, looking north-west. In mail-coach days this was the scene of delays in terrible snow-drifts. (Copyright: Aerofilms Ltd.)

Plate 6. Roman road 41c, north of Cirencester, coincident with modern road A417, which branches from the old straight line in the right foreground, leaving the former to continue as a minor road. This road linked Cirencester to Gloucester, 16 miles (26 km) distant, and was known as Ermin Street, not to be confused with Ermine Street, which ran northwards out of London (2a etc.) SP 020025 to NNW. (Copyright: Aerofilms Ltd.)

Plate 7. Foss Way (5e) at *Venonae,* a Roman settlement at High Cross, near Hinckley, Leics. SP 473886 to NNE. (Copyright: Aerofilms Ltd.)
Plate 8. The Portway (4b) in Hampshire. Caesar's Belt is in background, Streetley Copse to the left and Clap Gate at the bottom. SU 462523 to NE. (Copyright: Aerofilms Ltd.)

Plate 9 (Left). Roman road 82, linking Scotch Corner with Penrith, represented by the modern road A66 north of Richmond, North Yorks. (Copyright: Aerofilms Ltd.)
Plate 10 (Right). Stane Street (15) north of Slindon, West Sussex, dead straight, well raised and used as a bridle road. In the distance it continues towards Chichester under the A285 modern road. SU 952115 towards SW. (Copyright: Aerofilms Ltd.)

Plate 11. Vertical aerial photograph of Stane Street Roman road (15) at Tyrrell's Wood, near Leatherhead, Surrey. NNE is to the right. (Copyright: Aerofilms Ltd.)
Plate 12. The site of the Roman bridge that conveyed Stane Street (15) over the river Arun at Alfoldean, West Sussex. The original oak piles of Hadrianic date are preserved in two Sussex museums; those photographed here are modern. See also fig. 6 for a cross-section.

Plate 13. The *agger* of Stane Street (15) at Gumber Corner, near Bignor, West Sussex, with wide berm to left. Reference E. Curwen section 2, *Sussex Arch. Coll.,* 57, 137.
Plate 14. Stane Street (15) as a worn terraceway on Bignor Hill, West Sussex. SU 970128 to NW.

Plate 15. The Fen Road (25) passing through a golf course at Crickety Park, west of Peterborough, looking along the *agger* with side ditches. TL 141990 to NW.

Plate 16. The Fen Road nearer Peterborough as an inclined terraceway (see fig. 4) through Bluebell Walk Plantation. TL 150983 to NW.

Plate 17. A rare instance of preservation in the centre of a modern city: the low *agger* of Fen Road (25) passing beneath Butter Cross (the old market place) in Peterborough. Although a very subtle camber today, this feature can be seen much more clearly in photographs taken before 1900.

Plate 18. The Fen Road (25) further to the east in the Fens: Low Road, Whittlesey, a straight green lane. TL 256977 to W.

Plate 19. A minor modern road (B1145) on the line of a Roman road (38) near Bawdeswell, Norfolk. TG 039207 to W.

Plate 20. A branch of Roman road 38, running between Billingford, Norfolk, and Cowbit, near Spalding (380), is shown here as a farm road crossing the Peddars Way (33b). TF 798193 to E.

Plate 21. The same road (380) here properly called 'Roman Road', Moulton Chapel, Lincs, was formerly thought to be of twelfth-century origin on account of mentions in charters of that period as 'New Fendyke'. The chapel sitting on the line causes a northerly diversion of the modern road B1357. TF 292182 to E.

Plate 22. The present termination of Roman road 380 at Stonegate Road, Cowbit, Lincs. TF 261180 to W. This sequence of the name 'Roman Road' leading into 'Stonygate Road' occurs also in Luton, Beds (168a).

Plate 23. The *agger* of the Romanised Icknield Way near Chinnor, Oxon, the line being carried further on by the Lower Icknield Way (168b). The scale is in feet. SP 744007 to NW.
Plate 24. Half Moon Lane east, Dunstable, Beds, showing again the *agger* of 168a, which was followed by the old county boundary at one time. This photograph was taken in 1958 before road improvements.

Plate 25. Why it should have been necessary in modern times to block a four thousand years old right-of-way in this manner between Letchworth and Baldock is open to question. Nevertheless this was done by 1960 and meant a detour to follow the route (168a) further.
Plate 26. This view of the Romanised Icknield Way (168a) looking from Stump Cross towards Ickleton is more pleasant and shows the Way as a green lane on the county boundary between Cambridgeshire and Essex. Great Chesterford is less than one mile to the south.

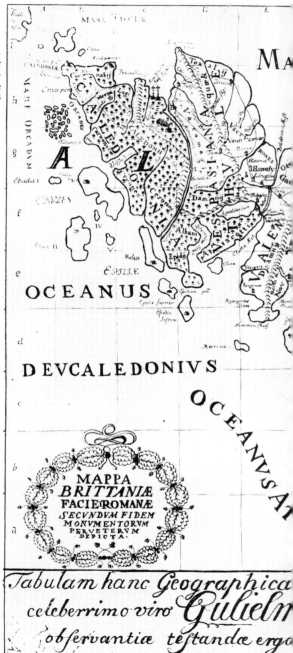

Plate 27. Genuine or clever fake? The arguments about this map of Roman Britain, executed by Charles Bertram in 1755, are discussed in the text. North is towards the left.

GALLIÆ BELGICÆ

GALLIA PARS

GERMANICUM.

GALLIÆ CELTICÆ PARS

Armoricæ civitates

VENETÆ

OCEANUS

MARE

TER=

MARE VERGIVUM.

BRITTANICUS.

Sinus Aquitanici Pars

NUM

VENNICNIJ

HYBERNII

CASSITERIDES

Pyrænæus Mons

=TICVS qui et BRITTANICVS

Antiquitatis Patriæ Cimélium
Stukeley. M.D.C.L.M.F.R.S.cet
D. Carolus Bertramus 1755.
C. Bertramus ipse delin: ab orig: & sculpsit.

Plate 28. The first portion discovered of a Roman road (173) between Dorchester-on-Thames and Alconbury House, a distance of 65½ miles (105 km) simply by investigating a place-name: Causeway End, Wootton, Beds. This is the *agger* at Keeley Green, taken in 1957. TL 010463 to NE.

Plate 29. A further portion of the same road (173a), showing the limestone metalling well scattered by ploughing alongside a footpath, the field being otherwise stone-free. Great Milton, Oxon. SP 628021 to NE.

Plate 30. The paved Roman ford at Kempston, near Bedford, in 1957, before the river Ouse flooded and destroyed much of it. Roman road 173c. TL 017477 to NNE.
Plate 31. From the same viewpoint looking back at the *agger*, metalling, oak piles and limestone slabs at the river's edge. TL 017477 to SSW. (Ref. *Beds Magazine*, 6, 57-60; see also fig. 6 for a cross-section.)

Plate 32. The remarkable *agger* in Claypits Field, Warden Street, now scheduled as an ancient monument, looking towards the Roman settlement at Shefford, Beds. Roman road 223. TL 127439 to SSE.

Plate 33. The same, looking from the opposite direction towards the hamlet of Warden Street and the radiused change of alignment at the field's end. TL 128435 to NNW.

Plate 34. After the alignment change, the minor modern road at Warden Street takes up the line for 500 yards (450 m). TL 127439 to NW.

Plate 35. Nettles are known to grow well on stony ground and where there has been human activity because of the acidity of the soil and excess nitrogen content. Here the *agger* of 210 near Henlow, Beds, is well covered. TL 159370 to N.

Plate 36. Looking along Gaddesden Row, Herts. This is a Roman road (169) on a pre-existing ridgeway with wide verges. The modern road exhibits slight warping and runs off-centre between the hedges on each side. TL 056124 to NW.

Plate 37. Roman road 169A looking towards Mentmore Towers, Bucks, in 1960. The line is preserved by the slightly raised modern road, but the verges are much too wide to be Roman and indicate later landscaping. SP 915181 to NW.

Plate 38. The Bound Way (177) as a raised green lane on a parish boundary by Bury Field, near Dunstable, Beds, in 1961, looking NE. This minor road linked Watling Street (1e) with the Romanised Icknield Way (168a) and passed through Streatley, Beds, accounting for this place-name. TL 004254.

Plate 39. All that remained in 1960, to the right of the photograph, of the Roman cutting through Puddlehill, Dunstable; 5 to 15 feet (1.5 to 4.5m) deep and estimated to be 20 feet (6m) wide, it eased the gradient of Watling Street (1e) at this notorious spot in the Chilterns. TL 003235 to SE.

Plate 40. The B660 modern road near Colmworth, Beds (Roman road 173d) in 1957 on a pronounced *agger* and with wide verges, looking north-east. TL 085569.

Plate 41. The B671 modern road at Bunkers Hill, Wansford, showing hump and wide verges (the Bullock Road extension to the river Nene) — almost the mirror image of the last picture. TL 078984 to NNW.

Plate 42. Bailgate and Newport Arch, Lincoln, looking north. Here the Ermine Street (2c) passes under the rear arch of the Roman north gate several feet below the modern road surface. The north part of the gate and west side passage are missing. The remaining portion was reconstructed in 1964 following a lorry accident.

Plate 43. Here at Water End in Hertfordshire the Roman road (169B) is not visible on the surface, but can be determined by the hump in the roof-line of the cottage built across it. TL 036106 towards WNW.

Plate 44. The B569 (Roman road 170) follows the county boundary between Bedfordshire and Northamptonshire southwards from the Roman town at Irchester down to this point between Wollaston and Podington, and then it becomes a green lane. This was one of John Ogilby's 'principal roads' in 1675. SP 922626 to S.

Plate 45. A possible continuation of Roman road 225 to Irchester along the parish boundary between Podington and Wymington, Beds, leads to this small paved ford at SP 935644.

Plate 46. A Coldharbour site. This one is at Ilmer, Bucks, on low lying ground (SP 757050). The associated Roman road is only tentative and may have passed through Henton to the south; the modern road there points either by design or accident at Bledlow Cross.

Plate 47. Gryme's Dell, Aldbury, Herts. Investigation of this place-name (meaning a ditch dug by the Devil, since according to the Anglo-Saxons it was too big to be man-made) was more fruitful. It revealed a Roman causeway (part of 169A) constructed across an iron-age ditch. The camber and metalling were unmistakable. SP 968119 to W.

Plate 48. An old rutted road at Dunstable, Beds, running parallel with the Romanised Icknield Way (168a) but near the town centre, as excavated by the Manshead Archaeological Society under L. Matthews in 1964. There was much Roman debris in the ruts and on top of the road. It could have been either a local Roman road or more probably Belgic in origin.
Plate 49. The old Roman road over Blackstone Edge, Greater Manchester (720a). A well-preserved portion of a paved road with central trough possibly used for retarding wheeled carts. (Copyright: Aerofilms Ltd.)

Plate 50. The *via principalis* at Usk, Gwent, in the centre of the Neronian legionary fortress. This section (scales in feet) shows second-century resurfacings and necessitates a revision of the line of Margary's road 612b. SO 397007 towards W. (Copyright: Dr W. H. Manning.)

Plate 51. Roman road 231 as it appears at the edge of a quarry near Bushmead Priory, Beds (section RWB 4). Appearances can be improved by cleaning up with a trowel and sprinkling water over the stony layers before photographs are taken. The horizontal datum is marked by a builder's line stretched at a convenient height.

Plate 52. The surface of a Roman road (which connects with the Bullock Road) revealed during aerial surveys carried out by Stephen Upex in 1974 and excavated under the direction of John Hadman in the years following. TL 048890 to W.

Plate 53. The same site (at Ashton, near Oundle) in 1976 with a second, wider road crossing the first. It was realised that a large Roman settlement existed here around these crossroads. TL 048890 to S.

Plate 54. Roman milestone at Chesterholm *(Vindolanda),* Northumberland. No inscription is visible today. (Copyright: David Wicks.)

Plate 55. Found amongst Roman road metalling at Ringshall, Bucks, this first-century AD corn mulling stone was made out of Hertfordshire conglomerate or 'puddingstone', Now in Luton Museum. SP 985144.

Plate 56. A trap for the unwary. Roman road 21b east of Hinxton, Cambs, marked by the A11 modern road on the left and not by the crop markings in the centre, which represent the course of a disused railway. TL 508455 towards SSW. (Copyright: Aerofilms Ltd.)

Plate 57. Another trap: a derelict road south-west of Ascot, Berks, 27 feet (8.2m) across, up to 2 feet (0.6m) high and metalled with sand and pebbles; a photograph taken in 1965. Sadly, I. D. Margary remembered its construction during the 1914-18 war, along with others in the same area. SU 908676 to SSE.

Index